this book is presented to:

_____

Bedtime Prayers

that end with a

hug!™

CREATED BY

Stephen Elkins

ILLUSTRATED BY

Ruth Zeglin

TYNDALE KiDS

Tyndale House Publishers, Inc.
Carol Stream, Illinois

Visit Tyndale's website for kids at www.tyndale.com/kids.

TYNDALE is a registered trademark of Tyndale House Publishers, Inc. The Tyndale Kids logo is a trademark of Tyndale House Publishers, Inc.

That End With a Hug!, *Share-a-Hug!*, the Share-a-Hug! logo, and *Share a Hug with Someone You Love* are trademarks of Wonder Kids.

Bedtime Prayers That End with a Hug!

Created by Stephen Elkins

Cover heart artwork copyright © Christina Veit/iStockphoto. All rights reserved.

Illustrated by Ruth Zeglin © Stephen Elkins. All rights reserved.

Designed by Jennifer Ghionzoli. Interior design Jennifer Ghionzoli and Jennifer Phelps.

Edited by Brittany Buczynski

For manufacturing information regarding this product, please call 1-800-323-9400.

ISBN 978-1-4143-8354-5

Printed in China

19	18	17	16	15	14	13
7	6	5	4	3	2	1

table of contents

Dear Parents and Grandparents,

This is a very special book about prayer. It encourages young children ages three through five to pray before bedtime. It defines what prayer is, who we are praying to, and 52 things that children can pray about—things as simple as saying "thank you" to God for all His blessings. Common fears, like thunderstorms and being afraid of the dark, are addressed. Best of all, as a parent or caregiver, you are encouraged to help grow this habit of prayer by showing your love and affection in the form of a hug after each bedtime prayer! In this way, your child will learn the importance of regular evening prayer and also be encouraged by your embrace.

A hug says, "I love you, I care for you, and I want God's best for you." These are *Bedtime Prayers That End with a Hug!* . . . and they can be the beginning of a lifetime of prayer!

Bedtime Prayers That End with a Hug! will help your child

- ♥ connect the prayer topics to the Bible
- ♥ understand that God speaks to us through the Bible and through prayer
- ♥ learn that prayer is a two-way experience—we talk to God and He speaks to us
- ♥ discover that the Bible is the best source for guiding us through our lives
- ♥ see that God is a real God (He's not imaginary) and that He is relevant
- ♥ learn that prayer should be a first response and not a last resort

This is indeed a special book because it seeks to glorify a special God who wants a relationship with your child. May each prayer you read, and each hug that comes with it, help to grow a strong and lasting faith in the life of your special child.

Stephen Elkins

♥ A Little Lamb's Prayer

A Prayer about the Shepherd

The LORD is my shepherd; I have all that I need.

PSALM 23:1

snuggle time

Shepherds know all about sheep. They know sheep are helpless and weak. They know sheep can't see very well and like to wander. That's why sheep need a shepherd to keep them safe.

Little lamb, do not fear.
The Lord, your Shepherd, is near!

bedtime Bible thought

David was a shepherd. As David watched over his sheep, he learned something. People are a lot like little lambs. Sometimes they are afraid. Sometimes they get lost. That's why David wrote, "The LORD is my shepherd." David knew that God would watch over him, just like a shepherd watches over a little lamb! God will watch over you, too!

my hug-a-bye prayer

Dear Father, I am Your little lamb! Watch over me tonight and keep me safe. I will not be afraid, because You are near. Thank You for being my Good Shepherd!

nighty night!

Give the one who prays to the Lord, our Good Shepherd, a great big

hug!

♡ Praise for Days
A Prayer to Thank the Lord

I will praise the
LORD as long as I live.

PSALM 146:2

Today and all my days,
I will give God all my praise!

♡

13

snuggle time

It's nice when someone sees your good work and thanks you for it. That's what praise is: seeing someone's good work and saying "thank you!" Praise is a good way to show love.

bedtime Bible thought

David looked up into the night sky. He saw the moon and all the shining stars God made. David praised God for who He was and for all He had done. God is happy when we praise Him for His good work!

 ### my hug-a-bye prayer

Dear Father, tonight before I go to sleep, I want to praise You. Thank You for who You are and for all You have done. You are an awesome God, and I PRAISE You!

 ### nighty night!

 hug!
time

 **Give the one who praises the Lord in prayer a great big**

hug!

 15

Precious to God
A Prayer about God's Love

You are precious to me
. . . and I love you.

ISAIAH 43:4

16

 ## snuggle time

Things that are PRECIOUS have great worth. Diamonds are PRECIOUS stones. Gold is a PRECIOUS metal. And you are a PRECIOUS child! You are a priceless treasure to your mom and dad. There's nothing more precious to them than you!

So precious am I that Jesus would die!

bedtime Bible thought

You are precious to your mom and dad. But you are even more precious to God. He showed what great worth you have by doing something your mom and dad couldn't do. God sent His Son, Jesus, to share His saving love with you! Children are so precious in His sight.

my hug-a-bye prayer

Dear Father, when I think of what You did to save me, I am amazed. How precious and loved You make me feel. Thank You, Lord, for Your saving love!

nighty night!

hug! time

Give the one who is precious to God a great big

hug!

The Worried Fisherman
A Prayer about Casting Cares

Cast all your anxiety on [God] because he cares for you.

I PETER 5:7, NIV

If you're worried, sad, or scared, talk to God and cast your cares.

Dad and I were going fishing. I watched what he did. First he put that squirmy worm on the hook. Then he swung the fishing rod back over his shoulder and . . . whizzzzz! He cast that fishing line way out into the water! Great cast!

bedtime Bible thought

Fisherman Peter tells us what to do with trouble. We "cast" it on God. It's like taking all our troubles, putting them on a fishing hook, and letting them go. Whizzzzz! Let's cast our cares far away into an ocean called God's love!

 ## my hug-a-bye prayer

Dear Father, sometimes I have troubles. But now I know what to do! I will cast my cares on You, just like Fisherman Peter did. Because You care for me!

 ## nighty night!

Give the one
who casts
their cares
on God
a great big

hug!

♥ My Stick-Tight Prayer
A Prayer that We Will Remember God's Word

Repeat [these commands] again and again to your children.

DEUTERONOMY 6:7

22

 ## snuggle time

Do you have a favorite song? How do you remember all the words? It's easy when you hear the song over and over again! When something is repeated, it sticks tight in our minds. That helps us to remember it.

Repeating what we hear God say
will help us learn His truth today!

bedtime Bible thought

Every day, listen as your parents talk about God and His mighty deeds. Learn as they talk about God's Son, Jesus. Soon the lessons of Jesus will stick tight in your heart and mind! So repeat God's Word again and again until it sticks tight!

my hug-a-bye prayer

Dear Father, I want Your Word to stick tight in my heart! Help me to listen and remember the lessons my mom and dad teach me about You. Be with my family and bless us!

nighty night!

hug!
time

♥

Give the one who wants God's Word to "stick tight" a great big

hug!

♡ Sisters and Brothers
A Prayer about Loving Others

Let us love
one another.

I JOHN 4:7, NIV

We show love by sharing, by caring, and by daring!

snuggle time

The word "love" has a lot of meanings. Some people say, "I LOVE ice cream!" because it makes THEM happy. But God's kind of love is more about making OTHERS happy. God's kind of love wants others to have some ice cream too!

bedtime Bible thought

How do we show God's love to others? We CARE about them, we SHARE with them, and we DARE to do nice things for them. It may be hard at first. But when we love one another, God is pleased!

 my hug-a-bye prayer

Dear Lord, help me to love others more. Help me to show Your love by SHARING more, CARING more, and DARING to do more for them. I love You, Lord.

 nighty night!

 hug! time

Give the one who loves others more each day a great big hug!

♥ Talking to God
A Prayer for Grandma and Grandpa

Pray for each other.

JAMES 5:16

snuggle time

Talking with grandparents can be lots of fun. You can tell them what you did today. They can tell you stories from long ago. When you are away from them, you can always ask God to watch over your grandparents. And God will surely hear that prayer!

God answers prayer anytime, anywhere!

bedtime Bible thought

Prayer is talking to God. You can pray about the things you need and the people you love. If your grandparents are well, ask God to keep them safe. If they are sick, ask God to help them get better. Start talking. God is listening!

 ## my hug-a-bye prayer

Dear Father, You tell us to pray for each other. Tonight I want to talk to You about Grandma and Grandpa. Please watch over them and keep them safe. I love them, Lord, and I know You love them too!

 ## nighty night!

hug! time

Give the
one
who talks
to God
a great big
hug!

♥ Happy Being Me
A Prayer of Happiness

I am fearfully and wonderfully made.

PSALM 139:14, NIV

God wants to see,
I'm happy with me!

snuggle time

It happens to all of us—we want to change the way we are.
We want to be smarter or prettier or stronger. But remember,
God doesn't make mistakes. He made you just the way you are.
You are wonderfully made! So be happy being you!

bedtime Bible thought

The Bible says that you are wonderfully made. God made you just the way He wanted you to be. So be happy being you! Don't try to be like someone else. God says YOU are wonderful!

my hug-a-bye prayer

Dear Father, I know You never make a mistake. You made me just the way I am for Your own special reason. Help me to be happy being me!

nighty night!

hug! time

Give the one who can say "I'm happy being me" a great big

hug!

 # The Wonders of Waiting

A Prayer about Being Content

Be content
with what you have.

HEBREWS 13:5, NIV

snuggle time

Some people are never happy. The more they get, the more they want. But others are content. They are happy with what they have. They trust God enough to wait for His best. God knows what you need. So be happy with what you have.

Be content and glad
with the things you have!

bedtime Bible thought

Being content doesn't mean you never want anything new. It means you're happy with what you have NOW. Why? Because what you have is what God has given! Be content today. And know that God has so much planned for you in the future!

 ## my hug-a-bye prayer

Dear Father, help me to be content. I believe that You know what I need and when I need it. You know best, so I will wait on You.

 ## nighty night!

hug! time

♥

Give the one who is content a great big hug!

♥ God Never Changes
A Prayer about Trusting God

I am the LORD, and I do not change.
MALACHI 3:6

Life rearranges, but God never changes!

snuggle time

Everything changes. The sunny summer weather changes to cool autumn days. People grow and change too. Sometimes we don't like the changes, like moving to a new house. But there is one thing that never changes: God!

bedtime Bible thought

Every year, the seasons change. Even your family might change. But God and His Word never change! Psalm 33:11 says, "The LORD's plans stand firm forever." God always stays the same. No matter what, God will always love you . . . and that will never change!

 ## my hug-a-bye prayer

Dear Father, I am so glad that You never change. I can always trust You to love me and watch over me. When things do change, Lord, help me to trust in You more!

 ## nighty night!

hug!
time

Give the one who believes that God never changes a great big

 hug!

♥ The Jesus Attitude
A Prayer for a Good Attitude

You must have the same attitude that Christ Jesus had.

PHILIPPIANS 2:5

"Attitude" is the way we think and act toward others. We should all want to have a GOOD attitude, by being kind and showing respect. Who has the best attitude of all? Jesus!

When attitudes get sour,
Jesus has sweetening power!

bedtime Bible thought

The Bible says we should have the same attitude as Jesus. He was HAPPY, so wear a smile. He was HELPFUL, so help others. He was HUMBLE, so put others first. Happy, helpful, and humble—now that's a Jesus attitude!

 my hug-a-bye prayer

Dear Father in heaven, help me to be happy, helpful, and humble like Jesus was. Forgive me, Lord, if I sometimes fail. I do want to be more like Jesus every day!

 nighty night!

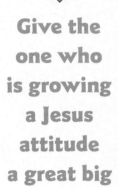

hug! time

Give the one who is growing a Jesus attitude a great big

 hug!

With All My Heart
A Prayer about Loving God

Love the LORD your God with all your heart.

DEUTERONOMY 6:5

Not just SOME little part,
God wants ALL my heart!

43

snuggle time

There's a big difference between giving SOME and giving ALL.
When you give SOME, you keep part of it for yourself.
But when you give ALL, there is nothing left to give.

bedtime Bible thought

The Bible tells us to love God with ALL our heart. God wants us to live for Him and not just ourselves. He isn't happy if we give Him just SOME of our love. We should love God with ALL our heart!

my hug-a-bye prayer

Dear Father, I want to love You with ALL my heart, not just some of it. Help me to be the kind of person You want me to be. I love You, Lord.

nighty night!

hug! time

Give the one who loves God with all their heart a great big

hug!

The Right Prayer Address

A Prayer Jesus Taught Us

Pray like this:
Our Father in heaven . . .

MATTHEW 6:9

46

snuggle time

My friend moved away. I wanted to send her a letter.
So I wrote her a note and mailed it. But my friend didn't answer.
Now I know why. I mailed the letter to the wrong address!

God's address has been given—
it's "Our Father in heaven"!

bedtime Bible thought

Jesus told us who we should pray to: OUR FATHER. God is called our Father because He made us, loves us, and takes care of us. Jesus even gave us God's home address: IN HEAVEN. So when we pray, let's be sure to have the right name and prayer address: OUR FATHER IN HEAVEN!

 my hug-a-bye prayer

Dear Father, You are OUR Father, not just mine. You are a Father to all Your people, everywhere. Our Father in heaven, thank You for listening to and answering all our prayers!

 nighty night!

hug! time

Give the one who prays to "our Father in heaven" a great big

hug!

♥ Do the Right Thing

A Prayer about Making
Good Choices

Choose today whom
you will serve.

JOSHUA 24:15

Choose God's way,
every day!

Joshua 24:15 choose today whom you will serve

49

snuggle time

Dad told me to never cross the busy street. But one day my friends started to cross. They wanted me to come too. "Come on!" they shouted. I had a choice to make: obey my dad or go with my friends. What was the right choice? Obeying my dad!

bedtime Bible thought

Joshua had a choice to make too. Would he honor the one true God or follow the bad, fake gods? Joshua made the right choice. He and his family chose to serve the one true God! To do the right thing, you have to make the right choice.

 ## my hug-a-bye prayer

Dear Father in heaven, help me to make the right choice, even when it's hard. Like Joshua, I want to always choose what honors You!

 ## nighty night!

 **hug! time**

Give the one who chooses to do the right thing a great big

hug!

♥ One, Two, Three, Forgive

A Prayer about Forgiveness

Lord, how many times shall I forgive my brother or sister . . . ? Up to seven times?

MATTHEW 18:21, NIV

52

snuggle time

My brother just won't leave my stuff alone! He says he's sorry, but he does it again and again. I try to forgive. But he is making it so hard! How many times do I have to forgive him?

To be like God in heaven, forgive seventy times seven.

bedtime Bible thought

Peter asked Jesus, "How many times should we forgive someone?" Peter thought seven times was plenty. He was surprised when Jesus said, "Forgive seventy times seven." Jesus meant we should always be ready to forgive!

 ## my hug-a-bye prayer

Dear Father, help me to forgive those who hurt me. Sometimes they do it again and again. I know You have asked me to forgive them. But it's hard. Help me, Lord, to forgive them, even 490 times!

 ## nighty night!

hug!
time

Give the one who is learning to forgive a great big

hug!

 54

The Daily Bread Prayer

A Prayer for Our Everyday Needs

Give us today our daily bread.

MATTHEW 6:11, NIV

Our God is able.
He puts bread on the table!

snuggle time

When I get hungry, I ask Mom for a snack. She takes out the bread and spreads on the peanut butter . . . yum! Sometimes I forget to say, "Thank you, Mom. And thank You, God, for giving us our daily bread!"

 ## bedtime Bible thought

Jesus taught us how to pray. We should thank God for who He is and ask Him for what we need: food, clothes, and a place to live. When we pray, "Give us today our daily bread," we are asking God to take care of us. This prayer reminds us that God alone gives us what we need and fills our tummies every day!

 ## my hug-a-bye prayer

Dear Father, please "give us today our daily bread." And thank You, Lord, for giving us what we need!

 ## nighty night!

Give the one who is thankful for daily bread a great big

hug!

♥ Love and Truth
A Prayer about Telling the Truth

Speak the truth in love.

EPHESIANS 4:15

snuggle time

Some things just go together, like peanut butter and jelly or cookies and milk. The Bible says that telling the truth goes together with something. Do you know what it is?

Speak truth in love,
like God above.

bedtime Bible thought

TRUTH and LOVE go together! Like a hand and a glove! It is always important to tell the truth. But we should never use the truth to hurt someone's feelings. We should speak the truth with love. These two things always go together!

 ## my hug-a-bye prayer

Dear Lord, You have taught us to tell the truth. But we must always tell the truth in love. Help us, Lord, to always speak with love as we speak the truth.

 ## nighty night!

hug! time

Give the one who tells the truth with love a great big

hug!

♥ Working for the Lord
A Prayer about Being a Good Worker

Work willingly at whatever you do, as though you were working for the Lord.

COLOSSIANS 3:23

Whatever work I do,
I do it, Lord, for You!

61

snuggle time

Dad said he needed my help. He was about to mow the grass.
My job was to pick up sticks in the yard. It was a little job.
But I wanted Dad to be happy with me. Because one day
he may ask me to do a bigger job!

bedtime Bible thought

Jobs come in many sizes. Some are small. Others take more time and skill. But whatever the job, you should do your best, as if you were doing the work for the Lord Himself. So always do your best!

my hug-a-bye prayer

Dear Father, help me to do my best whenever I am given a job to do. Teach me to work as if I am working for You.

nighty night!

Give the
one who
works as
if for
the Lord
a great big

♥ I've Got the Joy, Joy, Joy!
A Prayer about Being Joyful

Always be joyful.
1 THESSALONIANS 5:16

64

snuggle time

I was having a really bad day. Instead of smiling, I had a great big frown on my face. Mom said that I was her "little shining star" and she wanted to see my bright smile, not a frown! I laughed and smiled. She said that God wants us to be happy and joyful!

Let every girl and boy
be filled with lots of joy!

bedtime Bible thought

Everyone has a frowny face sometimes. But it doesn't have to stay that way. Joy comes from knowing that God loves you and you are special to Him! So if you ever start feeling grumpy, remember how much God loves you!

 my hug-a-bye prayer

Dear Father, sometimes I'm a little grumpy. Help me to remember that my joy comes from knowing that You love me and that I am special! Thank You, Lord. I love You!

 nighty night!

hug! time

Give the one with a joyful heart a great big

 hug!

Friendships Grow
A Prayer about Friendship

There is a friend who sticks closer than a brother.

PROVERBS 18:24, NIV

I have a Friend so dear.
He is always near!

67

snuggle time

Friendships start when you see someone often. Then friendships grow, and you become buddies. As you play and laugh together, sometimes a buddy becomes a BEST friend. You trust a best friend with your special secrets. But there is a Friend even better than that!

bedtime Bible thought

Solomon was the wisest man who ever lived. He said there is a Friend who is better than a brother. His name is Jesus! He's our heavenly Friend. Jesus does what no other friend can. He saves us!

my hug-a-bye prayer

Dear Father, thank You for Jesus. He is my closest Friend. No matter what happens, my heavenly Friend will help me. Thank You for this wonderful friendship with Jesus.

nighty night!

hug!
time

Give the
one whose
greatest
Friend
is Jesus
a great big

hug!

Thunder in the Heavens

A Prayer about Thunderstorms

I will comfort you.

ISAIAH 66:13

snuggle time

Are you afraid of thunder? Sometimes on a dark, rainy night,
thunder can be scary. It's so loud and sudden! But thunder
is a part of God's Creation. Thunder is just God's way of saying,
"Grab your umbrella. It's going to rain!"

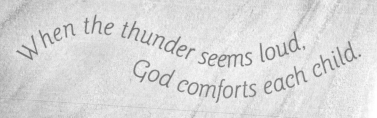

When the thunder seems loud,
God comforts each child.

bedtime Bible thought

Sometimes Isaiah was afraid too. But God comforted him. How does God comfort us? With promises! God promises to be with us in the storm. He will never leave us. So when we hear thunder crash, let's remember that God promises to take care of us!

 ### my hug-a-bye prayer

Dear Lord, when I'm afraid, help me to remember Your promises. You are with me and will never leave me, even when storms come.

 ### nighty night!

Give the one God comforts a great big

hug!

72

♥ Hide and Seek

A Prayer about Seeking the Lord

Seek first the kingdom of God.

MATTHEW 6:33, NKJV

Turn bored days into Lord days!

73

snuggle time

Everyone loves a game of hide-and-seek. First, some people run and hide. Then you have to find them. But unless you look really hard, you may never find them. That's why Jesus told us to SEEK the Kingdom of God.

bedtime Bible thought

Jesus wants you to seek God's best. But to find something, you have to know where to look! Where is God's best found? Look in the Bible! The Bible is where God tells you how to live. So open your Bible and seek God's best!

 ## my hug-a-bye prayer

Dear Lord, knowing You is the most important thing in this world. Lord, help me to put You first and to seek You always!

 ## nighty night!

♥ Trusting Enough to Wait

A Prayer for Patience

If we look forward to something we don't yet have, we must wait patiently and confidently.

ROMANS 8:25

snuggle time

There it was: the bicycle I had always wanted! I asked Dad if we could go inside the store to look at it. Dad said I needed to be patient because my birthday was just a few weeks away. Oh boy!

Be patient and rest.
Wait for God's best!

bedtime Bible thought

The Bible tells us we should wait with patience and confidence. "Patience" is being quiet and happy while we wait. "Confidence" is being sure that God will give us what we need. And He will give it at just the right time. So be patient. Trust God enough to wait.

 ## my hug-a-bye prayer

Dear Father, help me to trust You enough to wait! You know what is best for me and when is the best time for me to have it. And thank You, Lord, for being patient with me.

 ## nighty night!

 **hug! time**

Give the one whose patience is growing a great big hug!

A "Zoom Zoom" Prayer

A Prayer for Safe Travel

God is with you wherever you go.

JOSHUA 1:9

Near or far, here or there,
God is with me everywhere!

snuggle time

It was the first day of school. Soon the school bus would be here. I was so nervous and scared. But then Mom whispered in my ear. She told me that God would go with me and take care of me. I felt better right away.

bedtime Bible thought

Joshua knew that God is everywhere! There is no place you can go where God isn't there. God's promises are true everywhere—on a school bus, in a boat, or on the moon. As you travel, you can be sure God will be with you!

my hug-a-bye prayer

Dear Father, I'm glad that Your promises are true, no matter where I am. Thank You for keeping me safe at home, at school, and anywhere I may go.

nighty night!

hug! time

Give the one who is kept safe by the Lord a great big hug!

♥ A Generous Heart
A Prayer about Generosity

Blessed is he who is generous to the poor.

PROVERBS 14:21, ESV

snuggle time

Mom helped me put some of my clothes in a box. They were too small for me. So we were giving them to the poor. Mom said, "Some people may not have enough clothes to wear." Being generous is showing you care about others!

When we give to the poor, we give to the Lord!

bedtime Bible thought

Generous people like to give. That's because they care about others. They give their time by helping, their talents by serving, and their treasures by sharing what they have. Generous people care about others and do something to help!

 ## my hug-a-bye prayer

Dear God, help me to think less about what I want and more about how to help others. I want to be more generous!

 ## nighty night!

 ### hug! time

Give the one who wants to be generous to the poor a great big

hug!

Remember the Little Birds

A Prayer about Worrying

Look at the birds. . . . Your heavenly Father feeds them. . . . So don't worry about tomorrow!

MATTHEW 6:26, 34

Worrying today about tomorrow makes two days of sadness and sorrow!

snuggle time

I love watching little birds flutter around the bird feeder. They fly all around it, picking and pecking at their food. It's a favorite spot for the little birds. They look so happy! They don't seem to worry about anything. Why? Because God is taking care of them.

bedtime Bible thought

Jesus knew that worry doesn't change anything. What's the opposite of worry? Faith! Jesus taught that God takes care of the birds. You can trust Him to take care of you, too. Have faith!

 ## my hug-a-bye prayer

Dear Father, help me to remember the birds. They never worry. They trust You. Make me like a bird, Lord, so I will trust You every day.

 ## nighty night!

 hug! time

Give the one who chooses faith over worry a great big **hug!**

♥ It's like Visiting Jesus

A Prayer about Visiting the Sick

I was sick and you visited me.

MATTHEW 25:36, ESV

snuggle time

As we got in the elevator, I was a little scared. I'd never been in a hospital before. We were there to visit Grandma. When she saw us, she looked so happy! She had a great big smile on her face!

Lonely people pray for a visitor each day.

bedtime Bible thought

Jesus said that visiting someone who is sick is just like visiting Him! If Jesus were sick in the hospital, would you send Him a card or go visit Him? Well, now you know you can!

 my hug-a-bye prayer

Dear Father, please be with those who are sick in the hospital tonight. I want to visit the sick and show them Your love!

 nighty night!

hug!
time

♥

Give
the one
who will
soon visit
the sick
a great big

 hug!

♡ Talk about Everything

A Prayer about Talking to God

> Pray about everything.
> Tell God what
> you need.
>
> PHILIPPIANS 4:6

Nothing too big, nothing too small,
just pray to God about it all!

snuggle time

Do you like to talk on the phone? It's fun to talk to friends and family who live far away. But phone calls don't last very long. What's the most important thing to say?

bedtime Bible thought

Prayer is better than a phone call. When you pray, you can talk to God for as long as you want to. And you can talk about anything you want to. God has plenty of time. Nothing too big, nothing too small, just talk to God about it all . . . in prayer!

 ## my hug-a-bye prayer

Dear Lord, I am so thankful that I can talk to You about everything. There is nothing too big or too small to tell You about. Thank You for being a God who listens!

 ## nighty night!

hug!
time

Give the one
who talks
to God about
everything
a great big

hug!

♥ Excited to Tell
A Prayer about Sharing God's Greatness

Teach the law to anyone who does not know it.

EZRA 7:25

snuggle time

I was so excited! I couldn't wait to tell my friends! I was going to the circus, and I wanted everyone to know! That's what happened to Ezra. But it wasn't the circus he was excited about!

In Ezra's book we read
all about God's mighty deeds.

bedtime Bible thought

As Ezra studied God's Word, he got excited! He discovered just how great his God was . . . and he wanted everyone to know! So he told all the people about his almighty God. He even wrote a book. Let's all be like Ezra and tell others how great God is.

 ## my hug-a-bye prayer

Dear Father, I am excited to know how great You are! Give me the words to share Your story with others I meet. I love You, Lord!

 ## nighty night!

hug! time

Give the one who tells others about God a great big

hug!

A Light for My Path

A Prayer about God's Word

Your word is a lamp to guide my feet and a light for my path.

PSALM 119:105

Like a lamp shining bright, God's Word is my light!

97

snuggle time

It was very dark. Dad turned on his flashlight so we could see the path. I couldn't see all the way to the end of the road. But I could see where to safely step next.

bedtime Bible thought

The Bible is like a lamp. Without the light of God's Word, we might trip and fall. We can't see everything God has planned. So we stay in the light and take one step at a time. God's Word shows us where to go!

 ## my hug-a-bye prayer

Dear Father, thank You for Your Word. It is a light to my path. It shines the truth in a very dark and sinful world.

 ## nighty night!

hug! time

Give the one who lets God's Word light the way a great big

hug!

♥ My "Should Do" List
A Prayer about Praying Every Day

Lord, teach us to pray.

LUKE 11:1

 ### snuggle time

I have a "might do" list and a "should do" list. The "might do" list has things like riding my bike or playing with friends. I might do them, but not every day. The "should do" list has things I always do, like brushing my teeth . . . and praying!

Every night and day, always take time to pray.

bedtime Bible thought

Jesus had prayer on His "should do" list. He taught His 12 disciples the importance of prayer. Talking to God each day is not a "might do." It's a very important "should do." So be sure to pray every day!

my hug-a-bye prayer

Dear Father, I know I should start and end each day with prayer. But sometimes I forget! Teach me, Lord. Help me to keep prayer on my "should do" list!

nighty night!

hug! time

Give the one who is learning to pray each day a great big

hug!

♥ Life by the Numbers
A Prayer about Numbering Our Days

Teach us to number our days.

PSALM 90:12, NIV

Life is short, so every day,
do what's right and live God's way.

snuggle time

I was helping Mom put away a can of beans. The can's label said, "Use before March 20, 2015." Mom said the beans could not be eaten after that date. The beans' days had been numbered.

bedtime Bible thought

The Bible says God has numbered our days. Each day is a gift. So it's important to spend our days wisely and not waste them. Live for the Lord each day. That's numbering our days!

 ## my hug-a-bye prayer

Dear Father, teach me to number my days. Sometimes I waste the time You've given me. But, Lord, help me to remember how important each day is!

 ## nighty night!

 hug! time

Give the one who is learning to number their days a great big

 **hug!**

♥ Amazing Grace

A Prayer about God's Grace

No one can have greater love than to give his life for his friends.

JOHN 15:13, NLV

106

snuggle time

Dad had asked me to clean my room. How could I have forgotten? But when he saw how sorry I was, he gave me a big hug. He didn't give me what I really deserved. That's called GRACE!

Jesus gave His life, it's true, all to say, "I love you!"

bedtime Bible thought

God wants us to do more than keep a room clean. He wants us to keep our lives clean. But sometimes we forget. That's why we need grace! Jesus gave His life so we can receive AMAZING GRACE!

 ## my hug-a-bye prayer

Dear Father, Your grace is amazing! Because of Jesus, I can receive what I do not deserve: HEAVEN! Help me to remember that Jesus died for me. I want to live for Him.

 ## nighty night!

hug!
time

♥

Give the one who receives amazing grace a great big

hug!

♥ Good Fruit
A Prayer about Showing Kindness

Be kind
to each other.
EPHESIANS 4:32

Kindness, like honey, is sweet,
bringing smiles to those we meet.

 ### snuggle time

Oh no! I was running the bases when suddenly I tripped and fell!
Would everyone laugh at me? Coach Kelly came and helped me
up. He said with a smile, "It's okay. You gave your best, and
I couldn't ask for more!" His kind words made me feel better!

bedtime Bible thought

The Bible calls kindness a FRUIT OF THE SPIRIT. God wants to grow fruit in us! Not apples and oranges, but spiritual fruit—like love, joy, peace, and KINDNESS! That's God's kind of fruit!

 my hug-a-bye prayer

Dear Father, I know kindness is a fruit of the Spirit. It is something You help me grow. Help me, Lord, to be kind each day!

 nighty night!

 hug! time

Give the one who is kind a great big

 hug!

♥ In the Shelter of His Wings

A Prayer for Safety

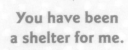

You have been a shelter for me.

PSALM 61:3, NKJV

Whether at home, school, or play, God shelters me every day!

snuggle time

There was a terrible rainstorm outside!
As we looked out the window, we could
see a mama bird snuggling her babies
under her wings. She was their shelter,
and her wings kept them safe.

113

bedtime Bible thought

God shelters us like that. A shelter is a place of safety! Our strong God keeps us safe in the storm. That's why David called God his shelter. David ran to Him in prayer when things got bad. We can do that too!

 my hug-a-bye prayer

Dear Father, I believe that You are real. Help me, Lord, to REALLY trust You. You have promised to shelter me. I will trust You, Lord, to do just that!

 nighty night!

 hug! time

Give the one God keeps safe a great big

hug!

♥ God Is Light

A Prayer about Being Afraid of the Dark

When you lie down, you will not be afraid.

PROVERBS 3:24, NIV

At night, do not fear.
Your heavenly Father is near!

GOD IS Light

snuggle time

The power had gone off. The house was very dark!
I couldn't see anything. It was so scary! Then Dad turned
on his flashlight. I wasn't scared anymore because I could
see my father was near.

bedtime Bible thought

A dark room can be a scary place. Maybe it's because we feel alone in the dark. But we're not. God is always there. We can talk to God in the dark of night or in the light of day. He's always with us!

 ## my hug-a-bye prayer

Dear Father, sometimes I am afraid. It gets very dark, and I can't see. Help me to remember that You are here with me! In those moments, Lord, be my light!

 ## nighty night!

 ## hug! time

Give the one whose God is light a great big

hug!

 **Be a Disciple**

A Prayer for Health and Strength

Fear the LORD and turn away from evil. Then you will have healing . . . and strength.

PROVERBS 3:7-8

My faith will start to grow
when discipline I show.

snuggle time

If you want to build strong muscles, you will need discipline. "Discipline" is not just knowing what to do. It's doing it every day! To grow stronger, you must eat good food and exercise every day! Does discipline build a strong faith, too?

bedtime Bible thought

Yes, discipline is how we build a strong faith! That's why Jesus' followers were called "disciples." They showed discipline by FEARING GOD, which means respecting Him. And they OBEYED GOD by doing what He asked. The disciples did these things EVERY DAY. That's discipline!

 ## my hug-a-bye prayer

Dear Father, I want to have a strong faith. Help me to respect You for all You've done. Give me a healthy body and a healthy spirit as I serve You every day!

 ## nighty night!

hug! time

Give the one who is growing a strong faith a great big

hug!

♥ Let Freedom Ring
A Prayer for Our Country's Leaders

Pray . . . for kings and all who are in authority.

1 TIMOTHY 2:2

Leaders take a country's care to a mighty God in prayer.

♥

121

snuggle time

There are two things every leader must have. First, a leader needs WISDOM. Wisdom begins by loving and respecting God. Then, a leader must have COURAGE to do what is right. WISDOM and COURAGE are the marks of a good leader!

bedtime Bible thought

In Bible times, most leaders were kings. Today, our country's leaders are the president and the Congress. And they need our help! How can we help? By praying for them each night! Ask God to give them WISDOM and COURAGE to be good leaders!

 ## my hug-a-bye prayer

Dear Father, please help those who lead our country. Give them wisdom and courage in all they do. We need You, Lord, to guide our country!

 ## nighty night!

 **hug! time**

Give the one who prays for our country's leaders a great big

 hug!

♥ Trust Has No Size Limit

A Prayer about Being Trusted

Whoever can be trusted
with very little can also
be trusted with much.

LUKE 16:10, NIV

 snuggle time

Our coach asked for a helper. I said I would do it. Before each
practice, I would set up the soccer net. So every Saturday
afternoon, I kept my promise! Our coach was proud of me!
He said I could be trusted to do a good job.

Trust is earned by being true
in what you say and what you do!

bedtime Bible thought

Doing a little job well builds trust. "Trust" means that people believe you will do what you say. Jesus said that if you can be trusted with a little, you can also be trusted with a lot. That's because trust has no size limit!

 ## my hug-a-bye prayer

Dear Father, I want people to trust me, too! I know trust is earned. Help me to tell the truth. Help me to do what I say. Help me, Lord, to be faithful to others, so everyone can trust me.

 ## nighty night!

hug! time

Give the one who can be trusted a great big hug!

♥ Rule Over Rover
A Prayer about My Pets

Rule over . . . every living creature that moves on the ground.

GENESIS 1:28, NIV

Be kind to little furry friends, for God loves and created them.

127

snuggle time

Dad let me get a puppy! I named him Rover.
Dad says someone needs to feed him and take him for
a walk every day. I guess that "someone" is me!

bedtime Bible thought

God created all the animals, and He asked us to "rule over" them. We should take good care of God's creatures—especially our pets. Let's "rule over" God's critters with a kind heart!

 ## my hug-a-bye prayer

Dear Father, my pet is so special to me. Help me to remember that pets were created by You. And You ask us to "rule over" them. Help me to love and care for Your Creation.

 ## nighty night!

hug! time

Give the one who "rules over" their pet with love a great big

hug!

♥ Let's All Say, "Obey!"
A Prayer about Obeying Parents

snuggle time

I'm just a kid. I don't know a lot about grown-up things.
So when my mom or dad asks me to do something,
I obey. I do it because they are wise and know what's
best for me. So I say, "Obey!"

God is pleased when children say,
"I am learning to obey!"

bedtime Bible thought

Did you know God has some special commands in the Bible just for kids? He wants kids to obey their parents in the Lord. Godly parents are wise. They love you and know what's best for you. So let's all say, "Obey!"

my hug-a-bye prayer

Dear Father, You have asked me to obey my parents. And that wasn't a suggestion. It was a command. So help me, Lord, to obey my parents with a glad heart!

nighty night!

hug! time

Give the one who obeys their parents a great big

hug!

♥ Meltdown Moments
A Prayer for Self-Control

Meltdown moments fade away
when you're self-controlled each day!

snuggle time

I didn't want to do it. But when she took my toy . . .
I got so mad! I started to cry and scream.
I had a meltdown moment! I'm so sorry!

bedtime Bible thought

Paul was a great Christian! But even he said, "I do things I don't want to do." Sometimes you lose control and do things you don't want to do. So ask God for self-control. It will stop your meltdown every time!

my hug-a-bye prayer

Dear Father, sometimes I do things I don't want to do. I get upset and have a meltdown. I know I need self-control, so I ask You to help me.

nighty night!

hug!
time

Give the one who asks for self-control a great big

hug!

♥ Hard Habit to Break

A Prayer about Changing
Bad Habits

I can do everything
through Christ.

PHILIPPIANS 4:13

 snuggle time

I had a very bad habit. I would eat breakfast and then off I'd go without brushing my teeth. Soon the dentist gave me the bad news. I had a cavity! Bad habits can have bad results!

To make bad habits go away,
ask God to give you strength today.

bedtime Bible thought

There's no bad habit God can't help you break. He's bigger than any habit. And He gives you this promise: with Him, you can do everything—even break that bad habit. Just ask Him in prayer!

 my hug-a-bye prayer

Dear Father, how great You must be.
You have made a promise, and I believe it.
I can do everything through Christ!

 nighty night!

hug! time

Give the one who can do everything through Christ a great big

hug!

♥ Who Can Out-Give God?

A Prayer about Giving

Please don't ever think it odd— you can never out-give God!

snuggle time

The missionary said people in Africa really needed water wells. And we could help! He asked us to give money so the people would have clean water. I gave my allowance money. Dad was proud of me!

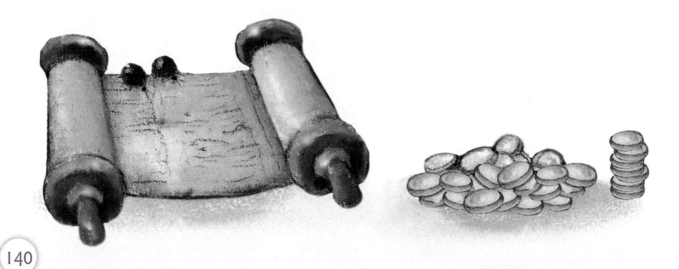

bedtime Bible thought

Like my dad, God is proud of us when we give. Being generous shows our love for people and our trust in God. And giving comes with a special promise: When we give to others, God will bless us! So be a generous giver!

 my hug-a-bye prayer

Dear Father, teach me to be a generous kid! Help me to give, knowing that You are proud of me when I do.

 nighty night!

hug! time

Give the one who is a generous giver a great big

hug!

Happy Endings
A Prayer about Reading the Bible

The Scriptures give us hope and encouragement.

ROMANS 15:4

Happy endings fill God's book,
so just open it and take a look!

I love a story with a happy ending! The bad guy has been doing all kinds of mean things. Then the hero arrives just in time and stops the bad guy. Hurray! The hero wins the battle! Did you know the Bible is full of happy endings?

bedtime Bible thought

My favorite "happy ending" is the story of Jesus. It looks like the devil is going to win. But then the hero, Jesus, is raised from the dead! What a happy ending! Let the Bible fill your life with happy endings too.

 ## my hug-a-bye prayer

Dear Father, thank You for the Bible. It is full of happy endings! Help me want to read my Bible more.

 ## nighty night!

 **hug! time**

Give the one who loves a happy ending a great big **hug!**

♥ Why Me, Lord?

A Prayer about Why
Bad Things Happen

In all things God works for the good of those who love him.

ROMANS 8:28, NIV

Though bad days bring sadness, God promises gladness!

145

snuggle time

Our pastor got hurt in a car crash. I couldn't believe it! He's a good man who loves God. He teaches us about Jesus every week. Why would God let such a bad thing happen to him?

bedtime Bible thought

Bad things do happen to good people. But why? Joseph found out the answer! His brothers sent him away. Then he was put in prison for something he didn't do. But the story wasn't over! God used Joseph to save His people. So trust God! Your bad days are working for good!

my hug-a-bye prayer

Dear Father, sometimes bad things happen to good people. When they do, help me to remember that the story isn't over yet. You are working everything for good!

nighty night!

Give the one who trusts God with bad days a great big

Going to the Doctor
A Prayer about Doctors

Don't be afraid,
for I am with you.
ISAIAH 41:10

148

snuggle time

I was so scared. I had to go see the doctor! What if I needed a shot? I hoped Mom would go in with me!

DOCTOR
OFFICE HOURS
ANYTIME

Doctors serve God too,
by taking care of you!

bedtime Bible thought

Doctors are God's helpers. One of Jesus' followers, Luke, was a doctor! When you get hurt or sick, doctors help you get well. So don't be afraid. Bring God to the doctor with you!

my hug-a-bye prayer

Dear Father, sometimes I'm scared of going to the doctor. Help me to remember that You are with me. Even in the doctor's office, I can trust You!

nighty night!

hug!
time

Give the one who brings God to the doctor a great big

Made Special to Be Special

A Prayer to God, Who Knows My Name

I have called you by name; you are mine.

ISAIAH 43:1

I'm special, I know, for God made me so!

MY Name IS ISAIAH

snuggle time

Every falling snowflake is special. No two snowflakes are the same. People are like snowflakes! There are millions of people in the world, but each one is different and special to God.

bedtime Bible thought

Unlike snowflakes, each one of us has a name. The Bible says that God knows your name! That's because He made you and He loves you. He also has a special plan for your life. You are made special to be special!

my hug-a-bye prayer

Dear Father, I am glad that You call me by name. You love me and have a special plan for me. Lord, You are special to me, too!

nighty night!

hug!
time

Give
the one
God calls
by name
a great big

hug!

♥ Two Powerful Words

A Prayer about Saying "I'm Sorry"

First go and make peace with your brother. Then come back and offer your gift.

MATTHEW 5:24, NIrV

snuggle time

Asking for forgiveness isn't easy to do. That's why I waited so long. But I went to my brother and told him I was wrong. Then I said, "I'm sorry." Those two little words changed everything!

Here's a lesson for everyone:
say "I'm sorry" when wrong is done.

bedtime Bible thought

Jacob had done a bad thing. He had taken something that belonged to his brother, Esau. So when Jacob saw Esau, he said, "I'm sorry." Those two little words made such a big difference! Esau forgave him!

 ## my hug-a-bye prayer

Dear Father, help me to say "I'm sorry" when I do something wrong. And keep me from doing it again! Thank You, Lord.

 ## nighty night!

 hug!
time

Give the one who is learning to say "I'm sorry" a great big hug!

♥ God Made Us All

A Prayer about Treating Everyone with Love

Treat everyone the same.

JAMES 2:1, NIrV

Treat everyone with love because God has made them one and all!

The basket shop was amazing. Each basket was a different color and size. The basket maker said he didn't have a favorite basket. He made them all, and he loved them all!

158

bedtime Bible thought

Jesus met a woman at the well. She was not a Jew. Most Jews refused to speak to her. But Jesus knew that she was loved by God, just like He was. So Jesus was nice to the woman. He talked with her and showed her God's love.

 ## my hug-a-bye prayer

Dear Father, help me to treat all people with love and respect. After all, You made each one, and You love each one. Thank You, Lord!

 ## nighty night!

 **hug! time**

Give the one who treats everyone with respect a great big

hug!

♥ Share-a-Prayer
A Prayer about Sharing

Share what you have, for [this is] pleasing to God.

HEBREWS 13:16, ESV

 snuggle time

As our teacher passed out the coloring pages, my friend looked sad. "What's wrong?" I asked. "I forgot my crayons," he said. "Don't worry," I told him. "You can share mine!" Sharing made us both happy!

Show God you care by learning to share!

bedtime Bible thought

Sharing is a good thing. A little boy once shared his lunch with Jesus. Jesus used that lunch to feed five thousand people! A little in God's hands goes a long way, doesn't it?

my hug-a-bye prayer

Dear Father, help me to share with others. I may not have a lot. But when I give what I have to You, it can go a long way!

nighty night!

hug! time

Give the one who is learning to share a great big

hug!

♡ Say It Out Loud

A Prayer to Say
"I Love You, Lord!"

I love you, LORD.

PSALM 18:1

Tell God as each day ends
how much you love your dearest Friend!

I LOVE YOU, LORD

snuggle time

Mom was putting dinner on the table. I wanted to tell her she was special to me. So I said, "Mommy, I love you!" Mom smiled. "What brought that on?" she asked. "I just wanted you to know," I said.

bedtime Bible thought

Sometimes you just have to say it out loud: "I love You, Lord!" You say it because you want Him to know how special He is to you. And when you say it out loud, He smiles too! Go ahead . . . make God smile!

 ## my hug-a-bye prayer

Dear Father, I love You! I hope hearing that makes You smile! Thank You for loving me, Lord, and always being near so I can talk to You. You are my dearest Friend.

 ## nighty night!

hug! time

Give the one who makes God smile a great big

 hug!

**Tape or glue a picture of your family on this page.
Remember to pray for them every day!**

♥ Special Bible Verses to Remember

In the beginning God created the heavens and the earth.
GENESIS 1:1

I am with you, and I will protect you wherever you go.
GENESIS 28:15

The heavens proclaim the glory of God.
PSALM 19:1

The Lord is my shepherd; I have all that I need.
PSALM 23:1

This is the day the Lord has made.
We will rejoice and be glad in it.
PSALM 118:24

Our help is from the Lord, who made heaven and earth.
PSALM 124:8

Thank you for making me so wonderfully complex!
PSALM 139:14

give a
Great Big
hug!

Bible Stories
that end with a
hug!™

CREATED BY
Stephen Elkins

ILLUSTRATED BY
Simon Taylor-Kielty

978-1-4143-7543-4

*From
MILLION-SELLING
author
Stephen Elkins*

Children love getting hugs as much as they love giving them!

Bible Stories That End with a Hug! features 74 timeless Bible stories, each with special verses and lessons on applying the Bible to your little one's life. And to make your time together an extra special event, each story ends with *a great big hug!*

share a hug with someone you love.™